Mastering the Art of Connection in Real Estate

Joel Erlichson

Copyright

Disclaimer

The information contained within this book is for general informational purposes only. While the author has made every effort to ensure the accuracy and completeness of the information provided, they make no guarantee regarding such. The author will not be held responsible for any errors, omissions, or inaccuracies in the information nor for any user's reliance on the information. The reader is responsible for their own decisions and should conduct their own research and seek the advice of professionals.

The opinions expressed within this book are the personal views of the author and do not necessarily reflect any legal or professional advice. The strategies discussed in this book are based on the author's personal experiences in the real estate industry and may not be suitable or applicable for everyone.

The reader is advised to assess their individual circumstances before implementing any strategy.

This book is not intended to serve as a replacement for professional advice or consultation. For legal, financial, or real estate advice, the reader should consult with an appropriate professional in their respective field.

Table of Contents

Chapter 1: Building Trust

1.1 The Importance of Authenticity

As realtors, we often find ourselves acting as the bridge between dreams and reality. Our clients entrust us with their aspirations of finding the perfect home or selling a beloved property, and our role is to navigate them through the complex, often intimidating process that lies ahead. In the midst of property tours, negotiation strategies, and closing deals, there's an element that is integral to the process but often overlooked: authenticity.

Authenticity is not just about honesty or transparency, though they are important facets of it. It's about presenting your genuine self to your clients, with all your strengths, passions, and even weaknesses. It's about being real and human in a field that's often seen as transactional and impersonal.

Perhaps you've experienced those moments where the conversation feels strained, where the connection seems superficial, and you're left wondering, "Why am I not clicking with this client?" Or maybe you've faced situations where you've given it your all, but the trust seems missing, the rapport non-existent.

These are challenges that many realtors face. And often, the root of these issues lies in the lack of authenticity. In an effort to maintain professionalism or to close a deal, we sometimes lose sight of our authentic selves. We resort to scripted dialogues, standardized pitches, and transactional conversations. But people sense that. They sense the lack of genuineness, and it can create a barrier.

Remember, when clients decide to work with you, they're not just buying a service; they're investing in you. They're placing their trust in your knowledge, expertise, and your ability to understand their needs.

They're relying on you to guide them through one of the most significant decisions of their lives.

By being authentic, you allow them to see the person behind the realtor. You let them know that you're not just there to make a sale, but to help them in their journey. You're not just an agent, but a partner, a guide. This authenticity is what builds trust, forges strong relationships, and ultimately, drives success.

So, as you navigate the world of real estate, embrace authenticity. Don't be afraid to be yourself, to share your experiences, to show your passion. Because in the end, it's not just about properties and transactions. It's about people, relationships, and trust. And there's nothing more authentic than that.

1.2 Active Listening: Key to Understanding Needs

As realtors, we've all been there. You're sitting across from a client, going over listings, discussing their options, but something seems off. You're doing all the talking, showcasing the best features of each property, trying to convince them, but the connection feels flat, even forced.

It might be easy to blame this on a tough client or perhaps, a mismatch in personalities, but often, it's not about them - it's about us. More specifically, it's about how we're communicating.

In our drive to prove our worth, to demonstrate our market knowledge and expertise, we often overlook a fundamental aspect of communication: listening. And not just hearing words, but truly listening – what we often refer to as active listening.

Active listening is more than just being quiet when the other person is talking. It's about being fully present in the conversation, absorbing not just the words, but also the underlying emotions, concerns, and aspirations. It's about understanding the unsaid, recognizing the hesitation in their voice, or the excitement in their eyes.

When clients come to us, they often carry a set of dreams, a list of needs, and a trunk full of anxieties. They might voice some of these, but many remain unsaid, hidden under the surface, waiting to be discovered. As realtors, our job is not just to sell them a property, but to unearth these hidden needs and address them. And that can only be done through active listening.

Active listening can feel challenging. After all, we're used to being the ones controlling the conversation, leading the discussion.

But the beauty of active listening lies in its simplicity. You're not expected to have all the answers or solve all the problems. You just need to be there, genuinely, attentively, actively.

By practicing active listening, you allow your clients to feel heard, understood, and valued. You build trust, foster a deeper connection, and often, uncover their true needs, the ones they didn't voice out loud.

In a world that's increasingly rushed and transactional, taking a moment to genuinely listen can set you apart. It can turn a standard client meeting into a meaningful interaction, a business transaction into a lasting relationship.

So next time you find yourself with a client, take a moment to truly listen. You'll be surprised by what you might discover. And more importantly, by how it can transform your relationship, and ultimately, your success as a realtor.

1.3 Transparency: A Pillar of Long-lasting Relationships

The real estate landscape can be daunting, complex, and for many of our clients, unfamiliar territory. The jargon, the market trends, the negotiations - they can all seem like a labyrinth that clients are expected to navigate. Often, this journey can lead to a sense of insecurity, a fear of the unknown. And that's where we step in.

But have you ever faced a situation where despite your best efforts, clients seem guarded? Or when they seem to doubt your suggestions, question your decisions? This is a challenge many of us face in the real estate field, and more often than not, the root of this issue is a lack of transparency.

Transparency isn't just about telling the truth. It's about letting clients into your world, allowing them to understand the process, the decisions, the complexities.

It's about making them feel a part of the journey, not just spectators or beneficiaries of the end result.

If you've found yourself in situations where that connection with your client seems to be missing, where trust seems to be a challenging bridge to build, it may be time to examine your transparency. Have you been openly sharing the process or simply presenting the outcomes? Have you been explaining your strategies or just implementing them?

Transparency builds trust because it removes the element of surprise. It allows clients to feel in control, to understand what's happening, and to actively participate in the process. This not only empowers them but also fosters a sense of partnership, of shared goals.

The real estate world, with all its twists and turns, can often feel like a closed book to clients.

As realtors, we have the opportunity to open this book, to demystify the process. This transparency in turn breeds confidence in your clients. They feel safer, more involved, and ultimately more connected to you.

So, if you're facing roadblocks in establishing strong, enduring relationships with your clients, take a moment to reflect on your transparency. Consider ways in which you can involve your clients more, explain processes better, and make your operations more visible. It's not just about sharing information; it's about opening up, letting your clients in, and building a bond of trust through transparency.

Remember, in a field where properties change hands, transparency is the real currency. It's what builds trust, forges connections, and leads to lasting relationships. And isn't that what being a successful realtor is all about?

Chapter 2: Showcasing Your Expertise

2.1 Be the Resource They Need

Picture this: a client steps into your office with a dream. Perhaps it's a young couple looking for their first home, a retired couple seeking a warmer climate, or an entrepreneur in search of the perfect commercial property. They have an idea, a need, but they're not quite sure how to turn it into a reality. They need a guide, a mentor, a resource. They need you.

But, have you ever felt like despite your best efforts, your clients still seem lost, confused, or overwhelmed? It's a common challenge many of us face in the real estate world. In our attempt to provide the best service, we sometimes forget to be the resource they truly need.

Being a resource isn't about knowing all the answers, but about knowing how to find them.

It's about guiding them through the complexities of the real estate market, making sense of the jargon, and providing them with the information they need, when they need it.

When clients come to us, they are not just looking for a realtor, but for an advisor, an advocate, and a confidant. They need someone who can decode the complexities of the real estate market, someone who can guide them through the decision-making process, someone they can rely on.

If you find yourself struggling to connect with your clients or meet their needs, take a moment to consider: Are you being the resource they need? Are you providing them with relevant, timely, and useful information? Are you guiding them, supporting them, and advocating for them?

By positioning yourself as a valuable resource, you not only enhance your professional image but also build trust with your clients.

They begin to see you not just as a realtor, but as a partner in their journey, a trusted advisor they can turn to.

So, the next time a client walks into your office, remember to be the resource they need. Share your insights, provide guidance, and most importantly, be there for them. After all, in the realm of real estate, being a trusted resource can be your most powerful asset.

2.2 Staying Current: The Importance of Continuous Learning

Imagine a scenario: you're at a listing presentation, and a client asks about a recent market trend or a new law affecting property transactions. Your mind draws a blank; you haven't heard about it yet. In the high-stakes world of real estate, situations like this can be a deal-breaker, making clients question your competency and tarnishing your reputation.

The real estate landscape is a vast, fast-changing field. New listings emerge every day, market conditions fluctuate, laws and regulations update, and client preferences evolve. As a realtor, staying abreast of these changes isn't just an added advantage - it's a necessity.

This concept of continuous learning might seem daunting. After all, you're already juggling various roles - negotiator, salesperson, counselor, and more. How can you add 'learner' to this ever-growing list?

Here's the thing - continuous learning isn't about stuffing your day with more tasks. It's about integrating learning into your routine, making it a natural part of your professional journey. It's about curiosity, adaptability, and a deep-seated passion for your field.

If you've been feeling out of touch, struggling to keep up with market trends, or finding it challenging to impress clients with your knowledge, it might be time to reevaluate your learning habits.

Are you staying current with the latest news, market trends, and legislation changes? Are you continually honing your skills, brushing up your knowledge, and pushing your boundaries?

As daunting as it might sound, the art of continuous learning can be your biggest ally. It keeps you relevant in a rapidly evolving field, equips you with the tools to serve your clients better, and distinguishes you as a proactive and dedicated professional.

Moreover, continuous learning doesn't have to be a solitary pursuit. It could involve networking with peers, attending seminars and workshops, participating in webinars, or even engaging in online communities. The goal isn't to know everything but to stay informed, to be in tune with the changes, and to never stop growing.

Remember, in the realm of real estate, your knowledge isn't just your power - it's your brand, your identity, your promise to your clients.

Staying current through continuous learning underscores your commitment to your profession, making you a more reliable, trustworthy, and, ultimately, successful realtor.

So, embrace continuous learning as your trusted companion in your real estate journey. Let it guide you, inspire you, and drive you towards a path of constant growth and unparalleled success. After all, when it comes to real estate, the learning never stops. And neither should you.

2.3 Positioning Yourself as an Authority

In the real estate industry, competition is fierce, and standing out can often feel like an uphill battle. As realtors, we all know the market, understand the transactions, and provide similar services. So, how do we distinguish ourselves in this crowded field? How do we command respect, gain trust, and ensure clients turn to us, and not others, for their real estate needs? The key lies in positioning yourself as an authority.

The term "authority" may seem like a heavy mantle, an accolade reserved for the elite few who have scaled the pinnacles of success. But in reality, becoming an authority is less about accolades and more about authenticity, less about superiority and more about service. It's about being the guiding light, the trusted source of knowledge, the one clients and peers look up to for advice, insights, and guidance.

If you're feeling lost in the crowd, struggling to make a mark, or finding it hard to connect with clients on a deeper level, it might be time to work on positioning yourself as an authority. This involves demonstrating your expertise, contributing to your industry, and forging a personal brand that stands for trust, knowledge, and integrity.

Demonstrating your expertise goes beyond just having the knowledge; it's about effectively communicating it to your clients and peers.

This includes explaining market trends, providing insights, answering questions, and proactively sharing valuable information. Your aim should not just be to sell properties, but to enrich your clients' understanding of the real estate world, transforming their journey from a transaction into an enlightening experience.

Contributing to your industry is another crucial aspect of becoming an authority. This could involve writing articles, giving talks, participating in panels, or engaging in community initiatives. Your goal here is not just to be a part of the industry, but to actively contribute to its growth, evolution, and enrichment. As you share your insights and experiences, you not only enhance your credibility but also give back to the community that shapes your professional life.

Finally, forging a personal brand is the cornerstone of your journey towards becoming an authority.

Your brand should reflect your values, your passion, your commitment, and your unique approach to real estate. It should tell a story, your story, and invite your clients to become a part of it. This creates a deep, lasting connection with your clients, making you more than just a realtor, but a trusted authority they can rely on.

Remember, positioning yourself as an authority is not an overnight process; it's a journey, a commitment to constant learning, growing, and giving. It demands dedication, authenticity, and a genuine love for your profession. But as you navigate this path, you will find that it not only enhances your professional standing but also enriches your personal growth.

So, take the leap, embrace the journey, and start positioning yourself as an authority. The real estate world is not just about transactions, listings, and commissions; it's about people, relationships, and trust.

And as an authority, you have the power to transform these transactions into relationships, these listings into dreams, and these commissions into trust.

In the end, remember, being an authority is not about standing above others, but standing with them, guiding them, and serving them. And in doing so, you not only elevate your career but also uplift those around you, shaping a more inclusive, enlightened, and enriching real estate landscape.

Chapter 3: Creating Value Beyond Transactions

3.1 The Art of Giving: Advice, Resources, and Time

There's a misconception that in the world of real estate, the deal is all that matters. We find ourselves in the pursuit of the next big sale, the next impressive commission, the next addition to our portfolio. We get so caught up in the transactions, the numbers, and the targets that we often overlook the most crucial aspect of our profession: people. And people are not about transactions, they're about connections, relationships, and values.

Creating value beyond transactions involves transforming your role from a realtor to a counselor, a confidant, and a friend. It involves stepping away from the sales pitch and stepping into the realm of authentic connection. It's about the art of giving - giving your time, your resources, and most importantly, your advice.

If you've been feeling a disconnect with your clients, struggling to forge lasting relationships, or finding it challenging to distinguish yourself in the highly competitive real estate market, it might be time to reflect on how you're adding value to your client relationships. Are you just helping them find a property, or are you helping them find a home? Are you merely closing a deal, or are you opening a chapter in their life story? Are you simply making a sale, or are you making a difference?

The art of giving, in the context of real estate, isn't about grand gestures or extravagant gifts. It's about lending an empathetic ear to your client's concerns, sharing resources that could help them make informed decisions, and dedicating your time to understand their needs, aspirations, and fears.

When it comes to giving advice, remember that your knowledge isn't just your power - it's your gift.

Share your insights about the market, provide guidance on property selection, and offer advice on negotiation strategies. But beyond that, advise them about the things that transaction details can't cover - the neighborhood culture, the potential for growth, the feeling of home. Show them that you're not just invested in their purchase, but also in their dreams, their comfort, and their happiness.

When we talk about giving resources, it's not just about property listings and market reports. It's about sharing resources that can aid their transition - be it a reliable moving service, a local home improvement store, or a handy neighborhood guide. It's about going the extra mile to ensure that their journey from property hunting to home owning is smooth, convenient, and enjoyable.

Lastly, giving your time is perhaps the most valuable gift of all. In our fast-paced world, time is the most precious commodity.

So, when you take out time to listen to your client's needs, to walk them through properties, to answer their queries, and to alleviate their concerns, you're not just giving them your time - you're giving them a piece of your life.

In essence, the art of giving is not a strategy or a tactic; it's a philosophy, a mindset, a way of life. It's about realizing that our role as realtors goes beyond just selling properties - it involves shaping experiences, building relationships, and impacting lives.

So, in your quest to succeed, remember to not just aim for more transactions, but also for more value. Remember to not just be a realtor, but also a giver - a giver of advice, resources, and time. Because, in the end, our success in the real estate industry is not defined by the number of properties we sell, but by the value we create, the relationships we build, and the lives we touch.

3.2 Problem-Solving: Your Biggest Value Proposition

In a world full of realtors, each vying for attention, each boasting of impressive portfolios and rich experiences, what sets you apart? What makes you the preferred choice for clients? What gives you that competitive edge? Your ability to solve problems could very well be your biggest value proposition.

If you've been wrestling with the challenge of differentiating yourself in the market or you're feeling overwhelmed by the pressure to continuously prove your worth, it might be time to shift your focus from selling to solving.

In the realm of real estate, problems are a constant. Clients grapple with a myriad of challenges - be it finding the right property within a budget, negotiating a fair deal, understanding complex contracts, or navigating through the maze of paperwork.

And these problems aren't just transactional or logistical; they're deeply personal. They involve their dreams, their security, their future.

In the midst of these challenges, you have the opportunity to become a problem solver. And being a problem solver isn't just about addressing the issue at hand; it's about taking a proactive approach, anticipating potential hurdles, and offering efficient, effective solutions.

Imagine you're a doctor, and your client is the patient. The patient doesn't just need a prescription; they need a diagnosis, an understanding of their condition, a treatment plan, and a guiding hand to help them through the recovery process. Similarly, your client doesn't just need a property; they need you to understand their requirements, evaluate options, devise a strategy, and guide them until they find their dream home.

Problem-solving also involves creativity. Every client is unique, with their set of needs, preferences, and challenges. Hence, the solutions you offer must be personalized, innovative, and flexible. It's about thinking outside the box, pushing the boundaries, and going beyond the conventional ways of doing things. It's about showing your clients that you're not just a salesperson, but a partner who's dedicated to making their real estate journey as seamless and successful as possible.

Furthermore, problem-solving enhances your value proposition. It positions you as a capable, reliable, and committed professional. It amplifies your credibility and fosters trust. It shows your clients that you're not just interested in closing a deal, but you're invested in their satisfaction, their comfort, their happiness.

So, if you're searching for that distinctive edge, that unique value proposition, look no further. Embrace the role of a problem solver.

Because, in the end, the real estate industry isn't just about properties, transactions, and commissions; it's about people, their problems, and your potential to solve them.

Remember, every problem is an opportunity in disguise - an opportunity to demonstrate your competence, show your empathy, and make a difference. So, don't just sell properties; solve problems. Because the latter doesn't just earn you a commission; it earns you respect, loyalty, and the reputation of a truly outstanding realtor.

3.3 Building a Business that Cares

In the bustling world of real estate, numbers often take precedence. Sale figures, market rates, commission percentages – they can quickly become the driving force behind your work. However, while these numbers are undeniably important, they cannot and should not become the heart of your business. The core of any successful business, especially one in the service sector like real estate, is care.

If you're a realtor grappling with creating a deeper connection with your clients, or if you're finding that despite good sales, your client relationships don't seem to last, it's time to step back and ask: "Am I building a business that cares?"

Creating a business that cares goes beyond delivering good service or closing successful deals. It's about embedding empathy, understanding, and genuine concern into every aspect of your business operations. It's about ensuring that every interaction your clients have with your business leaves them feeling valued, respected, and cared for.

A business that cares does not view clients merely as transactions. Instead, it sees each client as a unique individual with unique needs and aspirations. It seeks to understand these needs thoroughly and strives relentlessly to fulfill them. It acknowledges that behind every property purchase or sale, there's a person trying to build a better life, a better future.

Building a business that cares involves prioritizing client well-being over profits. It's about making decisions that are in the best interest of your clients, even if they might not be the most lucrative for you. It's about providing truthful, impartial advice and maintaining absolute transparency. It's about being a guide, a confidante, a friend – roles that are far more rewarding and meaningful than just being a salesperson.

A business that cares is also one that values relationships over deals. It understands that a one-time transaction might bring immediate gains, but a lasting relationship brings sustained success. It seeks to nurture these relationships with consistent communication, personalized attention, and unwavering support. It cherishes these relationships and holds them in higher regard than any sale or commission.

Moreover, a business that cares is committed to delivering exceptional client experiences.

It goes above and beyond to make the real estate journey enjoyable, hassle-free, and memorable for its clients. It pays attention to the minutest of details and leaves no stone unturned in ensuring client satisfaction.

In essence, building a business that cares is about adopting a holistic, human-centered approach to real estate. It's about making a shift from being sales-driven to being service-driven, from being profit-oriented to being people-oriented.

So, if you're looking to create lasting connections, to carve a unique niche, and to truly make a difference in your clients' lives, start building a business that cares. In the grand scheme of things, numbers may fluctuate, market trends may change, but care, concern, and genuine connections – they are timeless and invaluable.

Remember, at the end of the day, your success as a realtor will not be measured by the deals you closed but by the hearts you touched, the lives you bettered, and the difference you made. And that, in essence, is the power of building a business that cares.

Chapter 4: The Power of Networking

4.1 Cultivating a Robust Professional Network

In a hyper-competitive industry like real estate, having a high-performing professional network can be a game-changer. If you're a realtor who's been focusing primarily on traditional marketing methods and feeling like your career is stagnating, it may be time to shift your focus towards cultivating a robust professional network.

But what does having a robust professional network mean, and why is it so vital? In essence, a robust professional network is an ecosystem of relationships that provides support, fosters learning, offers mentorship, and often leads to opportunities that you wouldn't have discovered otherwise. A strong professional network is not just a collection of business cards from industry conferences.

It's a web of relationships built on mutual respect, shared interests, and professional reciprocity.

Creating such a network involves more than just attending networking events or becoming a member of professional organizations. It requires strategic planning, consistent effort, and, most importantly, a genuine interest in people. The secret to effective networking is to understand that it's not about getting; it's about giving. It's about adding value to your connections, sharing your expertise, offering support, and cultivating trust.

Networking isn't just about reaching out when you need a favor. It's about staying in touch regularly, following up, and showing genuine interest in your connections' lives and careers. It's about listening actively, understanding their needs, and offering your help in fulfilling those needs. It's about creating meaningful interactions that leave a lasting positive impression.

Furthermore, a robust professional network is diverse. It doesn't just include other realtors, but also mortgage brokers, contractors, interior designers, landscapers, legal professionals, and more. A varied network allows you to provide comprehensive solutions to your clients, increasing your value proposition. It also exposes you to different perspectives and ideas, enhancing your professional growth.

Building a strong professional network also involves maintaining an active online presence. Social media platforms, professional networking sites, online forums, and blogs offer excellent networking opportunities. They allow you to connect with industry professionals worldwide, participate in meaningful discussions, share your insights, and establish your authority.

Creating such a network requires patience and time, as meaningful relationships aren't built overnight.

However, the long-term benefits are invaluable. A robust professional network can help you gain referrals, stay updated with industry trends, broaden your skill set, improve your service delivery, and ultimately, amplify your success.

In conclusion, if you're a realtor looking to supercharge your career, start focusing on cultivating a robust professional network. Engage with your peers, participate in industry forums, leverage online platforms, and nurture meaningful relationships. Remember, the power of networking lies in the strength of the relationships you build and the value you provide to your connections.

Your success in the real estate industry is closely tied to the relationships you have with others. Networking offers a path to build these essential connections. By prioritizing networking, you're investing in a robust professional network that can support your career growth and open doors to new opportunities.

4.2 Referrals: Your Strongest Leads

Ask any seasoned realtor about their most potent source of leads, and there's a high chance their answer will be one word: referrals. If you're a realtor who's been heavily investing in cold calling or digital marketing but haven't been seeing the results you'd hoped for, it might be time to shift your focus to cultivating referrals.

Referrals are essentially word-of-mouth recommendations. They come from satisfied clients, trusted colleagues, or anyone who has had a positive experience with your services and feels confident enough to recommend you to others. But why are referrals considered such strong leads?

The reason is simple: trust. When a client comes to you through a referral, they're not just a lead; they're a lead that already has a level of trust in your capabilities.

This trust isn't because of a well-worded advertisement or a persuasive sales pitch, but because someone they respect vouched for you. In essence, a part of the trust-building process has already been done, and you can hit the ground running.

To cultivate referrals, it's crucial to provide service that's worth talking about. Yes, meeting client expectations is important, but if you want to be referral-worthy, you have to go above and beyond. You need to make each client feel like they're your only client, provide them with exceptional service, and make their real estate journey as seamless and stress-free as possible. When clients have such an experience, they naturally want to share it with others.

But providing exceptional service is just one part of the equation. The other part is communication. Often, realtors shy away from asking for referrals because it feels awkward or pushy.

But if you've provided great service and built a strong relationship with your client, asking for a referral should be a natural extension of your professional relationship.

This doesn't mean you need to blatantly ask for referrals. Instead, let your clients know that your business thrives on referrals and that you'd appreciate it if they could recommend your services to anyone in need. Also, remember to express your gratitude for any referrals you receive, regardless of whether they convert into business or not.

Moreover, consider setting up a referral program. Offering incentives can motivate your clients, colleagues, and other contacts to actively look for referral opportunities. The incentive doesn't have to be monetary—it could be a discount on future services, a small gift, or even a heartfelt thank you note.

Lastly, remember that giving referrals is as important as receiving them. When you refer clients to other trusted professionals, you're adding value to your clients, strengthening your professional relationships, and fostering a culture of reciprocity. The more you give, the more you're likely to receive.

To conclude, if you're a realtor looking to generate strong leads, start focusing on cultivating referrals. Strive to provide exceptional service, communicate effectively, give referrals, and create a referral program. Remember, in the world of real estate, word-of-mouth is golden, and referrals are, without a doubt, your strongest leads.

4.3 Collaborating to Achieve More

If you've been working as a realtor for some time, it's likely that you've come across the idea of "competition" more often than not.

While there's no denying that the real estate industry can be competitive, one of the most significant steps you can take to elevate your career is to shift your mindset from competition to collaboration.

In the real estate business, as with many other industries, the notion of the lone wolf, the singular, go-it-alone realtor, has been glamorized. However, the truth is that collaboration can offer a potent advantage in this field. If you've been feeling stuck, constantly racing against other realtors and feeling drained, it may be time to reframe your perspective and recognize the power of collaboration.

Collaboration means working together to achieve a common goal. In real estate, this could mean partnering with other realtors to co-list properties, share marketing efforts, or pool resources to offer better services to your clients.

It can also involve working with other industry professionals, such as home inspectors, appraisers, or mortgage brokers, to streamline the home buying or selling process for your clients.

The benefits of collaboration are multifold. Firstly, it allows you to leverage the strengths and expertise of others. Every professional has a unique set of skills, knowledge, and experiences. By collaborating, you can tap into this collective wisdom, offer more value to your clients, and learn from others.

Secondly, collaboration can help you reach a wider audience. When you collaborate with other realtors, your network, reach, and visibility expand. You get introduced to clients, contacts, and opportunities you might not have had access to otherwise. This can increase your lead generation and conversion, giving a significant boost to your career.

IFurthermore, collaboration fosters a sense of community. Instead of viewing other realtors as competitors, you start seeing them as allies. This shift in perspective can make your career more enjoyable, reduce stress, and lead to long-term professional relationships that can be incredibly rewarding.

Collaboration also extends beyond working with other realtors. Consider collaborating with local businesses, community organizations, or charities. Such partnerships can enhance your reputation, demonstrate your commitment to your community, and help you stand out.

The key to successful collaboration is to approach it with a mindset of mutual benefit. Collaborations shouldn't be one-sided; they should offer value to all parties involved. Be open, respectful, and willing to contribute as much as you gain.

In conclusion, if you're a realtor who's been stuck in a competitive rut, consider embracing the power of collaboration. Whether it's with other realtors, industry professionals, or your local community, collaborative efforts can enhance your service, extend your reach, and boost your career in ways you never imagined. Remember, in the realm of real estate, together we achieve more.

Chapter 5: Communication: A Deal Maker or Breaker

5.1 Mastering the Art of Persuasion

At the heart of real estate lies the art of persuasion. Persuasion is a powerful tool that is central not just to closing deals, but to every interaction and every relationship you cultivate in your career. However, mastering the art of persuasion is more than just knowing the right words to say or the right time to say them. If you're a realtor struggling to connect authentically, it might be time to delve deeper into the intricacies of persuasion and how to wield it effectively.

Firstly, let's dispel a common misconception: persuasion is not about manipulation. On the contrary, effective persuasion is based on honesty, understanding, and respect. It's about helping others see things from a different perspective, not tricking them into agreement.

So, how can you master the art of persuasion? It begins with empathy. Understanding your client's needs, worries, and desires is the foundation of persuasive communication. Empathy allows you to tailor your message in a way that resonates with your clients, addresses their concerns, and appeals to their aspirations. It's not about changing their minds, but about showing them how your proposition aligns with their interests.

Another vital aspect of persuasion is credibility. People are more likely to be persuaded by someone they deem trustworthy and knowledgeable. As a realtor, your credibility stems from your expertise, professionalism, and integrity. Continually updating your knowledge, adhering to ethical standards, and providing reliable service are crucial in establishing and maintaining your credibility.

Active listening also plays a key role in persuasion.

When you listen attentively to your clients, you show them that you value their thoughts and opinions. This not only gives you a deeper understanding of their needs but also fosters a connection that makes your persuasive attempts more effective.

Persuasion also requires clarity in communication. Be straightforward and concise with your message. Avoid jargon or overly complex language that could lead to misunderstanding. Remember, your goal is to help your client understand the benefits of your proposition, not to impress them with industry-specific terminologies.

Furthermore, non-verbal communication, such as body language, eye contact, and tone of voice, can significantly impact your persuasion efforts. Positive body language can convey confidence and sincerity, while maintaining eye contact can show attentiveness and respect. Meanwhile, a friendly and enthusiastic tone can make your message more appealing.

Lastly, remember that persuasion is a two-way street. Encourage dialogue, welcome questions, and be open to feedback. This not only makes your clients feel valued and heard but also gives you the chance to refine your persuasive efforts based on their responses.

In conclusion, mastering the art of persuasion can be a game-changer in your real estate career. It's not about manipulation, but about understanding, credibility, active listening, clarity, non-verbal communication, and dialogue. When wielded effectively, persuasion can enhance your communication, strengthen your connections, and undoubtedly be a deal maker in your real estate journey.

Lastly, remember that persuasion is a two-way street. Encourage dialogue, welcome questions, and be open to feedback. This not only makes your clients feel valued and heard but also gives you the chance to refine your persuasive efforts based on their responses.

In conclusion, mastering the art of persuasion can be a game-changer in your real estate career. It's not about manipulation, but about understanding, credibility, active listening, clarity, non-verbal communication, and dialogue. When wielded effectively, persuasion can enhance your communication, strengthen your connections, and undoubtedly be a deal maker in your real estate journey.

5.2 Clarity and Responsiveness: Non-negotiables in Communication

In the intricate dance of real estate, communication is the music that sets the pace.

It guides the steps, leads the direction, and often determines the outcome. However, communication in real estate is not merely a function; it's an art. And central to this art are two critical principles: clarity and responsiveness.

Clarity in communication is not just about speaking or writing well. It's about ensuring that your message is received and understood as intended. It's about eliminating ambiguity and reducing complexity. It's about presenting information in a way that makes sense to the receiver.

Why is clarity so critical? In the real estate world, miscommunication can be costly. A misunderstanding can lead to missed opportunities, protracted negotiations, or even a lost deal. Moreover, a client who constantly feels confused or misunderstood is likely to lose trust and confidence in their realtor.

As a realtor, you deal with a myriad of information: property details, market trends, legal requirements, financial terms, and so much more. Your ability to convey this information clearly and understandably to your clients is a testament to your expertise and professionalism.

Clarity also extends to your expectations, commitments, and feedback. Be clear about what you can deliver, what you expect from your clients, and how you perceive the situation. Honest and clear communication fosters trust, aligns expectations, and prevents disappointments.

Equally important as clarity is responsiveness. Responsiveness in communication is about promptness, attentiveness, and engagement. It's about showing your clients that they matter, that their concerns are important, and that you're there to support them.

A responsive realtor answers calls and messages promptly, addresses concerns quickly, and provides regular updates. They engage in active listening, empathize with the client's situation, and provide reassurance when needed. They are proactive in communicating, not waiting for the client to reach out first.

Responsiveness is more than just good manners; it's a demonstration of respect and reliability. A responsive realtor respects their client's time, worries, and aspirations. They understand that behind every question or concern is a person seeking a home, an investment, or a new beginning. A responsive realtor sends a powerful message: I see you, I hear you, and I'm here for you.

In the fast-paced world of real estate, where time can mean a difference of thousands of dollars or the perfect property, responsiveness is not just appreciated; it's expected.

In conclusion, clarity and responsiveness are non-negotiables in real estate communication. They are crucial in fostering trust, managing expectations, and providing excellent service. If you're a realtor struggling with making authentic connections, focus on improving your clarity and responsiveness. When your communication is clear and responsive, it becomes not just a tool, but a bridge - a bridge that connects you to your clients, your colleagues, and your success in real estate.

5.3 Emotional Intelligence in Negotiations

Emotional intelligence, the ability to understand, use, and manage emotions in positive ways, is a critical skill for realtors. It's what makes the difference between a transactional interaction and a genuine connection. And nowhere is this more evident than in negotiations.

The world of real estate can often be a high-stakes, high-pressure environment. As a realtor, you are entrusted with helping people make one of the most significant financial decisions of their lives. This responsibility, combined with the inevitable ups and downs of the negotiation process, can generate a whirlwind of emotions. And how you navigate through this emotional landscape can significantly influence the outcome of your negotiations.

If you've ever found yourself struggling to connect authentically during negotiations or have difficulty managing the emotional dynamics of these interactions, the concept of emotional intelligence may offer some valuable insights.

Emotional intelligence comprises several elements, each of which plays a vital role in negotiations:

Self-awareness: This is the ability to recognize and understand your own emotions and how they impact your thoughts and behavior. In a negotiation setting, self-awareness can help you identify your triggers, manage your reactions, and stay focused on your objectives.

Self-management: This refers to the ability to regulate and control your emotions, especially in stressful situations. In negotiations, maintaining composure, demonstrating patience, and staying optimistic, even when things are not going your way, can help keep the negotiation process constructive and forward-moving.

Empathy: This is the ability to understand and share the feelings of others. Empathy allows you to recognize the emotions of your clients, their concerns, fears, and aspirations. In a negotiation, showing empathy can help build trust, foster rapport, and facilitate understanding.

Social skills: These include skills in effective communication, building relationships, conflict management, and influencing others. Effective negotiators are not just good talkers; they are also good listeners. They respect others' viewpoints, seek win-win solutions, and influence not through pressure but through persuasion.

Enhancing your emotional intelligence can transform your negotiations from a contest of wills to a process of collaborative problem-solving. It allows you to go beyond the figures and the facts, to understand the people behind the numbers, and to find solutions that not only meet their financial needs but also their emotional needs.

Remember, every negotiation is not just about a property; it's about a dream, a future, a life. When you approach negotiations with emotional intelligence, you don't just close a deal; you open a world of opportunities for genuine connections and lasting relationships.

Therefore, as a realtor aiming to enhance your ability to make authentic connections, focusing on improving your emotional intelligence is a valuable investment. When emotions are managed effectively, they can be powerful allies in negotiations, turning potential conflicts into opportunities for understanding, collaboration, and mutual success.

Chapter 6: Leveraging Technology

6.1 Digitizing Your Business: Opportunities and Challenges

In today's digital age, technology has seeped into virtually every aspect of our lives, revolutionizing the way we communicate, work, and conduct business. The real estate industry is no exception. As a realtor, you may have noticed how technology has transformed the way you interact with clients, market properties, and even close deals.

Fully digitizing your business and leveraging technology to its fullest extent can be an overwhelming endeavor, presenting both opportunities and challenges.

Let's explore these facets.

Opportunities

1. Increased Reach: Digital platforms allow you to extend your reach far beyond traditional methods. Social media, digital advertising, and online listing platforms can expose your listings to a global audience, increasing visibility and potential buyer interest.

2. Enhanced Communication: Technology offers multiple channels for communication – emails, messaging apps, video conferencing, and more. This can make correspondence with clients more convenient and efficient, improving responsiveness and service.

3. Data-driven Decision Making: Digital tools can provide access to extensive real-time data about market trends, buyer behavior, and more. This information can guide your strategies, enabling you to make more informed, effective decisions.

4. Automation: From scheduling appointments to sending follow-up emails, automation can help streamline repetitive tasks, freeing up more time for you to focus on building relationships and closing deals.

Challenges

1. Privacy and Security: The digital realm brings with it concerns about data privacy and cybersecurity. As a realtor, you'll handle sensitive client information, and it's crucial to ensure this data is protected.

2. Technical Skills: Leveraging technology requires a certain level of technical know-how. Not every realtor is tech-savvy, and the learning curve might be steep for some.

3. Digital Overwhelm: The sheer volume of technology tools available can be overwhelming. Identifying which tools will truly add value to your business requires research, experimentation, and time.

4. Maintaining the Personal Touch: Real estate is a people business, and while technology can enhance communication, it should never replace the personal, human touch that's critical to building relationships.

Navigating the digital landscape can feel like a daunting task, especially if you're experiencing challenges in making authentic connections. However, remember that technology is simply a tool, a means to an end, and not an end in itself.

The goal of digitizing your business should not be to replace the human touch but to enhance it. To make communication more convenient, services more efficient, and relationships more robust.

As you journey through this digital revolution, approach it not just as a realtor, but as a problem-solver, a consultant, a partner.

Embrace the opportunities that technology offers, mitigate the challenges it presents, and above all, continue to prioritize authentic, meaningful connections with your clients. The art of connection, after all, is the true heart of the real estate business.

6.2 Online Marketing for Real Estate

In this era, the online world plays a crucial role in shaping consumer behavior and purchasing decisions, and real estate is no exception. Today, most property searches start online, and potential buyers and sellers are increasingly utilizing digital platforms for information, reviews, and recommendations.

If you've ever felt overwhelmed by online marketing, you're not alone. With ever-evolving algorithms, an abundance of platforms, and an influx of content, it can feel like navigating through a labyrinth. But remember, the core principle of online marketing mirrors the essence of being a realtor — it's all about building connections.

Building Your Digital Presence

The cornerstone of online marketing is a robust digital presence. It's more than just having a website; it's about creating an online hub where potential clients can get to know you, understand your services, and see the value you can offer. Include testimonials from satisfied clients, informative blog posts, and details about your unique approach to real estate transactions. You're not just marketing your business, you're creating a digital extension of who you are as a realtor.

Social Media

Social media platforms like Facebook, Instagram, and LinkedIn are valuable marketing tools. But instead of using them merely to showcase properties, use them to highlight your expertise, share insights, and engage with your audience. Remember, these platforms are social in nature; engagement and interaction are key.

A successful social media strategy is not about being active on every platform; it's about finding where your audience is and creating valuable content for them. It's about fostering a community and sparking conversations. You're not just selling properties; you're cultivating relationships.

Content Marketing

Content marketing involves creating and sharing informative, valuable content to attract and engage a target audience. Blog posts, e-books, infographics, and videos are examples of content you can create.

While it's tempting to focus solely on real estate-related topics, don't be afraid to venture into other areas that might interest your audience, like home decor tips, neighborhood guides, or mortgage advice. Your goal is not to just pitch your services but to become a go-to resource, a trusted authority in your field.

SEO

Search engine optimization (SEO) is the practice of increasing your website's visibility in search engine results. It's a complex, multifaceted process involving keywords, backlinks, quality content, and more. While mastering SEO takes time, even a basic understanding can help improve your website's ranking and visibility.

Email Marketing

Even with the emergence of new platforms and tools, email remains a highly effective marketing channel. An email newsletter can keep you in regular contact with your audience, providing them with insights, updates, and personalized content.

Even with the emergence of new platforms and tools, email remains a highly effective marketing channel. An email newsletter can keep you in regular contact with your audience, providing them with insights, updates, and personalized content.

Online marketing might seem like a technical endeavor, but at its core, it's a medium for storytelling. It's an opportunity to tell your story, share your expertise, and engage with your audience. It's a platform to provide value, solve problems, and build relationships.

So, if you're a realtor grappling with the challenge of building authentic connections, consider reframing your approach to online marketing. Don't see it as a daunting task, but an exciting opportunity to connect, engage, and add value. Remember, at the heart of every like, share, comment, or click is a person, seeking connection, advice, or solutions. And as a realtor, you are well-equipped to provide just that.

6.3 Tools to Boost Efficiency and Productivity

When you're a realtor, every day is a whirlwind.

From meeting clients to staging homes, from closing deals to managing paperwork, it can often feel like there's a mountain of tasks to conquer, and just not enough hours in the day. The good news? Technology can be your best ally. It can help you streamline processes, manage time effectively, and boost productivity. The key is to find the right tools that cater to your specific needs and fit seamlessly into your workflow.

CRM Systems

One of the most important tools in your arsenal as a realtor is a good Customer Relationship Management (CRM) system. CRMs are designed to help you manage all your relationships and interactions with current and potential clients. A good CRM can help you track your leads, schedule follow-ups, and monitor your deals. It's like your own personal assistant, helping you stay organized and on top of your game.

Now, there's a common misconception that CRMs are complex and intimidating. But the truth is, they're designed to make your life easier. So, if you're a realtor who's struggling with managing client relationships and staying organized, consider investing in a CRM. It might take some time to learn and adapt, but the benefits are well worth the effort.

Digital Marketing Tools

We've already established the importance of online marketing in the previous section. But managing multiple social media accounts, regularly updating your website, and creating engaging content can be time-consuming. That's where digital marketing tools come into play.

From content management systems and social media schedulers to email marketing platforms and SEO tools, there's a wide range of software designed to simplify your digital marketing efforts.

They help automate repetitive tasks, provide insightful analytics, and free up your time to focus on what you do best - building connections.

Virtual Tour Software

In today's fast-paced, digital world, offering virtual tours is no longer a novelty; it's a necessity. Virtual tour software allows you to create immersive, interactive experiences that allow potential buyers to explore properties from the comfort of their homes. It's a powerful tool to attract and engage prospects, and a great way to stand out in the competitive real estate market.

Productivity Apps

In the midst of meetings, viewings, and negotiations, it's easy to overlook the smaller tasks - the ones that silently pile up and cause stress. Productivity apps can help you manage these tasks efficiently.

They help automate repetitive tasks, provide insightful analytics, and free up your time to focuFrom note-taking apps and project management tools to time trackers and to-do lists, there's an app for almost every productivity challenge you might face. The key is not to use them all, but to identify the ones that address your specific needs and integrate them into your daily routine.

E-signature Platforms

In the real estate industry, paperwork is a necessary evil. But with e-signature platforms, you can simplify the process significantly. These tools allow you and your clients to sign documents electronically, saving time, reducing errors, and speeding up transactions.

The realm of tech tools can seem overwhelming, especially if you're not particularly tech-savvy. But remember, these tools are not meant to add complexity; they're designed to simplify, streamline, and enhance your work.

So, if you're a realtor finding it hard to juggle various tasks, or if you're struggling to keep up with the digital age, consider exploring these tech tools. They won't replace the personal touch and authentic connection that define your role as a realtor. But they can provide you with the time and space to focus on what truly matters - connecting with your clients and serving them better.

Chapter 7: Learning from Success, Failure, and Everything in Between

7.1 Navigating Challenges: Strategies for Problem-Solving in Real Estate

Every realtor encounters roadblocks in their career. From difficult clients and sudden market shifts to internal pressures and tough negotiations, the real estate business is filled with challenges that can test even the most seasoned professionals. And let's face it: no matter how well you've planned, things won't always go smoothly. It's how you handle these challenges that will define your career and shape your reputation in the industry.

What if we reframed these challenges? What if, instead of viewing them as insurmountable obstacles, we saw them as opportunities for growth and learning? That's what problem-solving in real estate is all about. It's about adopting a resilient mindset and leveraging strategic thinking to navigate complex situations.

But how can we foster such a mindset? And what strategies can we apply to solve problems effectively?

Adopt a Solution-Focused Mindset

The first step in navigating challenges is adopting a solution-focused mindset. When faced with a problem, it's natural to dwell on the issue, to dissect it, to let it consume us. But often, focusing too much on the problem can cloud our judgment and impede our ability to find solutions.

Instead, shift your focus. Try to envision the outcome you desire and work backwards from there. Ask yourself: What actions can I take to achieve this outcome? What resources do I have at my disposal? Who can I reach out to for assistance or advice?

Analyze and Understand the Problem

Understanding the problem is key to finding effective solutions.

Take the time to analyze the situation thoroughly. Gather as much information as possible and aim to understand all aspects of the problem. Look at the issue from different angles and perspectives.

Are you dealing with a client who's reluctant to commit? Are market conditions not in your favor? Is there a communication breakdown with a colleague? Once you've identified the crux of the problem, you can start crafting a strategic plan to address it.

Leverage Your Network

Remember the saying, "No man is an island"? That's particularly true in real estate. You're not alone in your challenges. There are countless other realtors who've been in your shoes, who've faced similar problems and have found ways to overcome them.

Reach out to your professional network. Seek advice from mentors, colleagues, or industry peers. Join online forums or real estate groups where you can share your experiences and learn from others.

Stay Informed and Adaptable

The real estate industry is constantly evolving, and with it, the nature of the problems you'll encounter. Staying informed about market trends, technological advancements, and industry best practices can help you anticipate potential challenges and devise effective strategies to tackle them.

But it's not just about staying informed; it's about being adaptable. It's about being willing to change your approach, learn new skills, and step out of your comfort zone.

Remember, challenges are part and parcel of the real estate business. But with a solution-focused mindset, a good understanding of the problem, a strong network, and a commitment to continuous learning and adaptability, you can navigate any challenge that comes your way. And with each problem you overcome, you'll not only grow as a realtor but also strengthen the authentic connections that are the cornerstone of your success.

7.2 Embracing Failure: It's Part of the Process

Real estate is not for the faint-hearted. As a realtor, you may have experienced the high stakes, the heart-racing negotiations, and the ever-present possibility of a deal falling through at the last minute. We have all faced failure at some point in our careers, and it's never easy. It can be discouraging, demoralizing, and downright painful. But, as counterintuitive as it may seem, failure can be one of our greatest teachers if we let it.

The truth is, in the unpredictable world of real estate, failure is part of the process. It's not a sign of incompetence or a mark of shame; it's an opportunity to grow, learn, and build resilience. Embracing failure and learning from it is integral to becoming a successful realtor.

When a deal goes south or a client relationship crumbles, it's natural to feel disappointment. Allow yourself to feel these emotions, but don't let them consume you. Instead, make a conscious effort to shift your perspective and embrace these failures as stepping stones on your journey to success.

Reflect on why you failed. Was it a communication breakdown? Were there market factors you didn't account for? Did you misjudge a negotiation? Identifying what went wrong can help you pinpoint areas for improvement.

It can also shed light on what you could do differently next time. Remember, the goal isn't to avoid future failures - that's an unrealistic expectation - but to learn how to navigate them better.

Embracing failure also involves cultivating a culture of openness and transparency around setbacks. Too often, there's a stigma attached to failure in professional settings. But sharing your experiences - the good and the bad - can build trust and authenticity, especially in client relationships. Clients value honesty. Admitting that you don't have all the answers, that you too make mistakes and learn from them, can actually enhance your credibility.

Moreover, shared stories of failure and recovery can be powerful connectors, not only with clients but also with your peers. These stories remind us of our shared human experiences, of our shared struggles and triumphs. They help us understand each other better, fostering stronger, more authentic connections.

Perhaps most importantly, embracing failure cultivates resilience. In real estate, resilience - the capacity to recover quickly from difficulties - is a crucial asset. Deals will fall through. Clients will be difficult. The market will fluctuate. It's those who can face these setbacks head-on, learn from them, and bounce back who will stand the test of time in the real estate industry.

So the next time you find yourself facing a failure, remember: it's not a dead-end but a detour on your path to success. Embrace it. Learn from it. Share your experience and show your resilience. Not only will this help you become a more successful realtor, but it will also allow you to form deeper, more authentic connections with those around you.

7.3 The Power of Resilience

In the world of real estate, one quality often sets successful agents apart from others - resilience.

Resilience is the ability to bounce back from setbacks, adapt to change, and keep going in the face of adversity. It's about weathering the storm and coming out on the other side stronger and more determined.

As a realtor, you are constantly navigating uncertainty. Market trends can change overnight, promising deals can fall through, and clients can be unpredictable. The unexpected is just part of the job. It's during these trying times that resilience becomes your most valuable attribute.

It's natural to experience disappointment and frustration when things don't go as planned. You may question your abilities, your strategies, or your decisions. While these moments of doubt are part of the process, it's essential not to get stuck in this mindset.

Instead, try viewing challenges as opportunities for growth and learning. What can this situation teach you? Perhaps it's a new approach to negotiations, or maybe it's a better understanding of a particular market segment. Every challenge presents an opportunity to learn something valuable about your profession or yourself.

Don't hesitate to seek support during difficult times, either. Building a network of mentors, peers, and industry professionals can provide a much-needed sounding board. These connections can offer advice, share their own experiences, and provide reassurance when you're navigating tough situations.

Remember, resilience isn't about masking your emotions or pretending everything is okay when it's not. It's about acknowledging the struggle and choosing to focus on your ability to overcome it.

It's about demonstrating to your clients that no matter the adversity, you are someone who can navigate through it and still deliver the best possible results. This resilience not only makes you a better realtor, but it also fosters a deeper sense of trust and respect with your clients.

Resilience is not something you're born with; it's something you build over time. With each hurdle you overcome, you become a little bit stronger and a little bit more resilient. It's an ongoing journey, not a destination.

In the end, it's the resilient realtors who thrive. They can weather the market's ups and downs, navigate challenging client relationships, and turn failures into learning opportunities. They're the ones who are not just surviving in the industry, but truly flourishing.

So when you face your next challenge – as you inevitably will – remember the power of resilience. Embrace the opportunity to learn, to grow, and to strengthen your resolve. Your resilience is your superpower, and it's what will carry you through the toughest times and help you succeed in the end.

Chapter 8: Planning for the Long Haul

8.1 Building a Sustainable Business Model

If you've made it this far into our journey together, then you've already developed a strong foundation of trust, expertise, value, networking, communication, technological savviness, and resilience. These elements are not only keys to immediate success but also building blocks for a sustainable business model in real estate. A model that doesn't burn you out or leave you chasing after the next commission, but one that stands the test of time, weathers market fluctuations, and allows for your continued growth and satisfaction in this dynamic industry.

What does a sustainable business model look like in real estate? The specifics may vary based on market conditions, geographic location, and personal strengths, but there are some common characteristics.

At its core, a sustainable business model in real estate is client-centric. It prioritizes the long-term satisfaction and success of your clients over the quick close of a deal. This client-first approach builds strong, lasting relationships that can provide a steady stream of referrals and repeat business.

Next, sustainability is about balance. As realtors, we can often fall into the trap of being "always-on," feeling the need to respond to every email, call, or text immediately, regardless of the time of day or what else might be happening in our lives. But for the sake of your wellbeing and the quality of the service you provide, setting boundaries is vital. This may mean setting specific business hours, taking regular days off, or outsourcing certain tasks that are not the best use of your time.

Furthermore, a sustainable business model leverages technology. Not for technology's sake but to improve efficiency, increase reach, and deliver better service.

This might include a CRM to manage relationships, a robust online presence to attract and nurture leads, or virtual tour capabilities to provide convenience for out-of-town clients.

It also considers financial sustainability. This means diversifying your income streams where possible, keeping overheads low, planning for lean times, and regularly reviewing your pricing strategy. Is your commission structure competitive? Are you maximizing the value you provide to justify your fees?

Lastly, a sustainable business model is adaptable. The real estate market is continually evolving, as are the needs and preferences of buyers and sellers. Regularly reassess your strategies, keep up-to-date with industry trends and shifts, and be willing to pivot when necessary.

Remember, building a sustainable business model doesn't happen overnight. It takes time, reflection, and often a bit of trial and error. But with patience and perseverance, you can create a business that not only survives but thrives in the long haul. One that allows you to do what you love – connecting with people and helping them navigate one of the most significant transactions of their lives – in a way that is rewarding, balanced, and sustainable for many years to come.

8.2 The Power of Consistency

Every seasoned professional, regardless of their field, understands the potency of consistency. As realtors, this principle is no different. Success in our line of work is rarely a result of a single, massive effort, but rather a series of small, consistent actions repeated over time. Consistency is the not-so-secret weapon that can help us build stronger relationships, establish credibility, and maintain a steady stream of business.

Let's think about this. Imagine you are a potential client seeking a real estate professional to help with your property transaction. Would you prefer an agent who sporadically communicates, irregularly updates their market knowledge, and seems to be continually trying new approaches, or an agent who steadily and reliably communicates, consistently stays up-to-date, and exhibits a stable, dependable strategy?

Therein lies the power of consistency in our profession. It breeds familiarity and trust, making potential clients more comfortable in choosing you as their representative. Furthermore, regular, consistent action helps you build a strong personal brand and reputation.

Yet, consistency is not just about repeating the same thing over and over.

It's about maintaining a high standard of service, an unwavering commitment to your clients' best interests, and a steady approach to your personal and professional development.

For instance, consider your communication with clients. Establishing a pattern of clear, timely communication from the get-go sets the stage for a productive working relationship. This doesn't mean bombarding clients with unnecessary updates, but rather keeping them informed about their transaction's significant aspects.

In the same vein, consistent learning and skill development are critical. The real estate landscape is dynamic and ever-evolving. Regularly updating your industry knowledge, market insights, and technical skills ensures you stay ahead of the curve, offering the best possible advice and service to your clients.

Consistency in networking and marketing efforts is equally important. These activities are not one-off tasks to be ticked off a list but ongoing endeavors that require regular attention. It's not just about making a contact or sending out a marketing piece once; it's about nurturing those relationships and creating a consistent brand presence over time.

Even when things don't go as planned, remaining consistent in your approach can help you navigate setbacks and challenges. Real estate is a business filled with ups and downs, but maintaining a steady, consistent approach to your work can help you weather the inevitable storms.

In the end, consistency may not be the most glamorous aspect of our work, but it is one of the most impactful. It's the steady rhythm that underpins every successful real estate career.

If you are struggling to connect authentically or feel overwhelmed by the constant hustle, consider focusing on the power of consistency. It might just be the missing piece you need to take your real estate career to new heights.

8.3 Adapting to Market Changes

The real estate market is as dynamic as it is exciting. Trends shift, interest rates fluctuate, and new regulations are continually shaping the landscape. Amid this ever-changing environment, the ability to adapt quickly to market changes is an essential attribute for a successful realtor.

Let's be clear: adapting to market changes is not about chasing every new trend or abruptly shifting your business model every time the wind changes direction. Rather, it's about maintaining a keen understanding of the market and being nimble enough to adjust your strategies when necessary.

To thrive in real estate, you must become a student of the market. This requires continuously staying abreast of industry news, tracking local and national market trends, and understanding the factors that influence property prices. Whether it's a sudden shift in housing demand, a change in mortgage rates, or the introduction of new real estate laws, you should be knowledgeable enough to explain these changes to your clients and guide them accordingly.

Adapting to market changes also means reassessing your strategies and tactics regularly. What worked phenomenally well a year ago may be less effective today. For example, if you've always been successful with open houses, but suddenly they're not generating the same interest, it may be time to pivot. Perhaps, virtual tours are gaining more traction in your market, or maybe private, scheduled showings are now the norm. Being flexible and open to trying different tactics is a crucial part of staying competitive.

Equally important is adjusting your communication and negotiation strategies in response to market shifts. In a buyer's market, your negotiation approach will be different than in a seller's market. Being able to recognize these shifts and adapt your tactics accordingly can be the difference between securing a deal or losing one.

Another key aspect of adapting to market changes involves technology. With advancements in digital tools and platforms, the way we do business is continually evolving. Embracing these changes can enhance your efficiency, reach, and service quality. Whether it's leveraging social media to reach potential clients, using virtual tour software to showcase properties, or adopting a CRM to manage your client relationships, staying technologically adaptable is key.

In conclusion, adapting to market changes isn't about being reactive; it's about being proactive.

It's about anticipating shifts, preparing for them, and using them as opportunities to better serve your clients and grow your business. By maintaining this adaptability, you can ensure your real estate business remains resilient and successful, no matter what the market throws your way.

Conclusion: Your Journey Ahead

As we close this guide, it's essential to remember that you are embarking on a journey. Becoming a successful realtor doesn't happen overnight. It's a journey marked by persistence, continuous learning, relationship-building, and adaptation to changing landscapes. Most importantly, it is a journey paved with authentic connections and genuine service to your clients.

Your journey as a realtor isn't solely about the number of homes you sell or the commissions you earn. It's about the relationships you cultivate, the trust you build, and the value you bring to people's lives. It's about helping people find a space they can call 'home' or selling a property that signifies a significant phase in their lives. The true measure of your success lies in the satisfaction of your clients and the positive impact you have on their lives.

The advice and strategies outlined in this book are not rigid rules but rather guiding principles to help you navigate your journey more effectively. Each chapter is designed to inspire you, challenge you, and equip you with practical insights to become not just a good realtor, but a great one. Remember, every successful realtor has faced challenges, made mistakes, and learned invaluable lessons along the way. What separates the great from the good is their ability to learn from these experiences, adapt, and continually strive for excellence.

As you move forward, keep your clients' needs and interests at the forefront of everything you do. Be their trusted advisor, their problem-solver, and their advocate. Harness the power of networking, master the art of communication, and leverage technology to improve your service and efficiency.

Adapt to market changes, stay consistent, and build a sustainable business model that can weather any storm. Remember, your journey is unique, and your path to success may differ from others. Stay true to your authentic self, and success will follow.

Your journey as a realtor is just beginning. It's a journey that promises growth, challenges, and a great deal of satisfaction. Embrace it with an open mind, a willing heart, and an unwavering commitment to serve your clients the best you can.

The road ahead is exciting, and the opportunities are vast. Go out there, make authentic connections, create value beyond transactions, and become the best realtor you can be. Your journey awaits. Safe travels.